Leo's Letter to the Church's of America

God's Righteousness

By

C. Leo Young, Jr.

authorHOUSE

1663 LIBERTY DRIVE, SUITE 200
BLOOMINGTON, INDIANA 47403
(800) 839-8640
www.authorhouse.com

First published by AuthorHouse 07/30/04

ISBN: 1-4184-5917-8 (e)
ISBN: 1-4184-2582-6 (sc)

Printed in the United States of America
Bloomington, Indiana

This book is printed on acid-free paper.

Table of Contents

Introduction:

I've written this letter to prepare the way for the message to the church's of America. My plan is to work among the Christians and to visit in the name of the Son, Our Lord Jesus Christ. **I've written to you** as a servant, an apostle, chosen to preach the good news. The message is God's powerful way of saving all people who have faith in His Son Jesus.

I am reminding my readers, all of us have sinned and fallen short of God's glory. But how can we be made acceptable to God? This is the main question answered in this letter about the believer having peace with God and being set free by God's Spirit from the power of sin and death. **The Jews have not obeyed** the law of God and the **Gentiles have refused** even to think about God, although God has spoken to them in many different ways. Wrestle with the question of how Jews and Gentiles fit into the plan of God for mankind.

Now we see how God makes us acceptable to Him. God treats everyone alike. He accepts people only because they have faith in Jesus Christ...God is kind! Because of Jesus Christ, He freely accepts us and sets us from our sin.

God gave Christ to die for our sins and He raised Him to life so that we would be acceptable to God.

My Prayer

God our Father in the name of Jesus Christ our Lord, renew our spirits and our heart to Thyself, that our work may not be to us a burden but a delight and give us such love to Thee as may sweeten all our obedience. Help us that we may serve Thee with the cheerfulness and gladness of children, delighting ourselves in Thee and rejoicing in all that is to the honor of Thy name, Jesus Christ.

O Lord Jesus through the power of your Holy Spirit You enable us to do and be more than we can think or imagine. Come now, dwell within us and make us strong to do Your work and will.

O Lord Jesus Christ You have shown me what it means to be a servant. I ask now for Your grace and strength to faithfully follow in the footsteps of servanthood. Almighty God and Father of America, *may the transforming of Your gospel be at work in my life and be written today and always.*

Leo, A Servant of Jesus Christ

God chose me to be an apostle and He appointed me to write and preach the good news. This good news is about His Son, our Lord Jesus Christ. But the Holy Spirit proved that Jesus is the powerful Son of God because He was raised from death.

Jesus was kind to me and chose me to be a writer and apostle, so that people of all nations would obey and have faith. You Americans are some of those people chosen by Jesus Christ.

This letter is to all of you in America. God loves you and has chosen you to be His very own people.

I pray that God our Father and our Lord Jesus Christ will be kind to you and will bless you with peace.

Leo called himself a servant, obeys the command of Jesus the chief among His apostles should be the servant of all. **America, Good News is about a risen Savior** from the grave, the long promised Christ completed the eternal plan to save believers. This proved that Jesus is the Son of God who could die for our sins. He is a living Savior.

Jesus chooses believers, instead of our choosing Him. Someday we will understand better what Leo writes here and in other places about that. For now lets be humble enough to accept the idea that God has had us in mind for a very long time.

A Prayer of Thanksgiving

I thank God in the name of Jesus Christ for all of you. I do this because people everywhere in the world are talking about your faith. God sees how I never stop praying for you while I serve Him with all my heart and tell the good news about His Son.

In all my prayers, I ask God to make it possible for me to visit you. I want to see you and share with you the same blessings that God 's Spirit has given me. Then you will grow stronger in your faith. What I am saying is that we can encourage each other by the faith that is ours.

American, My friend, I want you to know that I have often planned to write but something has always kept me from doing it. I want to win followers to Christ in America. It doesn't matter if people are civilized and educated or if they are uncivilized and uneducated.

I must tell you, I am eager to write all of you in America. **Leo prays** a lot and so should you. **God sees to it** that our prayers for one another make a difference. Often the best thing we can do is pray for the needs of others, especially for things when we can't help ourselves. **Only God can convince people that they need Christ.** Our words alone won't do it, but prayer makes a difference.

American, Good news about Jesus is not only for the "civilized and educated," but for the "uncivilized and uneducated." **The good news** is for people regardless of their importance in the world. We must be careful not to make the good news hard for people to understand. Even small children should be able to come to Jesus and be saved.

Chapter 1
The Power of the Good News

America:

Leo, for I am not ashamed of the gospel, for it is the power of God for salvation to everyone who believes, to the Jews and also the Gentiles. The good news tells how God accepts everyone who has faith, but only those who have faith. It is just as it is written, **"But the righteous man shall live by faith." "The people God accepts because of their faith will live."**

America's faith is trusting what God has said about His Son. Faith says, **"Accept Jesus as our**

Savior and we ask Him to take away our sins of the land of America." For the first time America realize what real living is like - when God breathes His own life into us. Without faith, America lives a life of sin, rebellion and death.

Everyone is Guilty

American, from heaven God shows how angry He is with all the wicked and evil things that sinful people do to crush the truth. **They know** everything that can be known about God, because God has shown it all to them.

America, God's eternal power and character cannot be seen. But from the beginning of creation God has shown what these are like by all He has made. **That's why** those people don't have any excuse.

They know about God, but they don't honor Him or even thank Him. Their thoughts are useless and their stupid minds are in the dark. **They claim** to be wise, but they are fools. **They don't** worship the glorious and eternal God. **Instead they worship** idols that are made to look like humans who cannot live forever and like birds, animals and reptiles.

America, so God let these people go their own way. **They did** what they wanted to do and their filthy thoughts made them do shameful things with their bodies. **They gave** up the truth about God for a lie and **they worshipped God's creation instead of God, who will be praised forever.**

American, God let them follow their own evil desires. Women no longer wanted to have sex in a natural way and **they did** things with each other that were not natural. Men behaved in the same way. **They stopped** wanting to have sex with women and had strong desires for sex with other men. **They did**

shameful things with each other and what has happened to them is punishment for their foolish deeds.

American, since these people refused even to think about God, He let their useless minds rule over them. That's why **they do** all sorts of indecent things. **They are** evil, wicked and greedy as well as mean in every possible way. **They want** what others have and they murder, argue, cheat and are hard to get along with. **They gossip**, say cruel things about others and hate God. **They are** proud, conceited and boastful, always thinking up new ways to do evil.

American, these people don't respect their parents. **They are** stupid, unreliable and don't have any love or pity for others. **They know God has said** that anyone who acts this way deserves to die. But they keep on doing evil things and they even encouraged others to do them. **Americans know that God's law says** that people who live in this way deserve death.

4

Yet not only do they continue to do these very things, but they even approve of others who do them.

America, what happens when we reject God? Because those people refuse to keep in mind the true knowledge about God, He has given them over to corrupted minds so that they do that which they should not do. When we reject God everything else goes wrong too.

American, this lists the things that happen in our lives when we turn our back on God. The picture human behavior paints is an ugly one indeed. The tragedy is that it is all so needless. **God is calling Americans back** from this "wrong turn" to enjoy friendship with Him. **The people God accepts** will live because it is written, **"The righteous will live by faith."**

Chapter 2
God's Judgment Is Fair

American, some of you accuse others of doing wrong. But there is no excuse for what you do. When you judge others, you condemn yourselves, because you are guilty of doing the very same things. We know that God is right to judge everyone who behaves in this way based on truth as it is written.

American, do you really think God won't punish you, when you behave exactly like the people you accuse? You surely don't think much of God's wonderful goodness or of His patience and willingness to put up with you. **Don't you know** that the reason God is so good to you is because He wants you to turn to Him. **America, do you** realize that God's kindness leads you toward repentance.

American, you are stubborn and refuse to turn to God. **So you are** making things even worse for yourselves on that day when He judges the world with fairness. **God will** reward each of us for what we have done. **God will** give eternal life to everyone who has patiently done what is good in the hope of receiving glory, honor and life that lasts forever. **God will show** how angry and furious He can be with every selfish person who rejects the truth and wants to do evil. **For those who are** self-seeking and who reject the truth to follow evil, there will be wrath and anger.

American, all who are wicked will be punished with trouble and suffering. It doesn't matter if they are rich or poor, Jews or Gentiles.

American, all who do right will be rewarded with glory, honor and peace, whether they are Jews or Gentiles. God doesn't have any favorites!

American, people who don't know about God's law will still be punished for what they do wrong. And the law will be used to judge everyone who knows what it says. God accepts those who obey His law but not those who simply hear it.

American people naturally obey the law's commands, even though they don't have the law. This proves that conscience is like a law written in the human heart. **America, it will** show whether we are forgiven or condemned, when God has Jesus Christ judge everyone's secret thoughts just as my message says; "It is written."

American, my friend, do you pass judgment on others? You have no excuse at all, whoever you are. For when you judge others and then do the same things which they do, you condemn yourself. **Jesus Christ is the judge for everyone. For it is** not by hearing the law that people are put right with God, but by doing what the law commands us to do as it is written.

American, how God judges by His law. If God judges us according to what we deserve, then there is no hope for any of us. **God offers** another way for us to be accepted by Him. Everyone has sinned and the law can only condemn us. **Americans, God** has made it possible for us to come back to Him and have our sins forgiven. People still cry, "What must I do to be saved? How can I be saved?" **The Bible provides a clear answer. America this good news is Six Scriptural Steps to Salvation. "As it is written."**

The Jews and the Law

Americans, some of you call yourselves saved. **You trust** in the commandment and take pride in God. **Americans** by reading the scripture you learn and discover what is right. **You are** sure that you are a guide for the blind and a light for all who are in the dark. **And since** there is knowledge and truth in God's commandment, you think you can instruct fools and teach young people.

American, how can you teach others when you refuse to learn? **You preach** that it is wrong to steal, but you steal. **God says people** should be faithful in marriage. But are you faithful? **You hate** idols, yet you rob their temples. **You take** pride in the commandment but you disobey the commandment and bring shame to God. **It is** just as the scriptures tell us **"You have made foreigners say insulting things about God."**

America, first it is written because of you the name of God is blasphemed among the Gentiles.

American, being religious is worthwhile if you obey the rules. **But if you** don't obey the rules, you are no better off than people who are not religious. **In fact**, if they obey the rules, they are as good as anyone who is religious. **So everyone who obeys the rules**, but has never been religious will condemn you. Even though you are religious and have the rules, you still don't obey its teachings.

American, just because you live like a Jew and are religious does not make you a real Jew. To be a real Jew you must obey the rules. True religion is something that happens deep in your heart, to have praise from God and not from humans.

American, the real Jew is the person who is a Jew on the inside, that is whose heart has religion and that is the work of God's Spirit, not of the written rules. **Such a person** receives his praise from God, not from man.

American, being religious, we are an example of disobedience. The Americans had the scriptures and they knew the rules. **They even** became very proud of these facts. **But they** were really no better than other people. They too failed to keep God's rules. **America there is danger** that people can imagine that they are good just because they know what they should do. **But they** don't do what they should, so their knowledge does them no good.

American, part religion can't cover our sins. Americans have many religious ceremonies. **But God** couldn't accept their religious ceremonies without obedient lives. **Today's Christians** might count too much on ceremonies, too. **Sometimes** children enjoy playing church, but it's sad when grown ups "play church" and aren't living and worshipping in a way that pleases God.

American, "I asked you, what can we do in order to do what God wants us to do?" They answered, What God wants you to do is to believe in the one He sent." **The one** came down from heaven to do the will of the Father who sent Him. **His name is Jesus our Lord and Servant.**

American, Jesus said I am telling you the truth, each one of you must turn away from his sins and you must be baptized in the name of **Jesus Christ**, so that your sins will be forgiven; and you will receive God's gift, the Holy Spirit. **Jesus said**, He is the Way, the Truth and the Life; no one goes to the Father except through Me.

Chapter 3
God's Faithfulness

American, what good is it to be a Jew? What good is it to be religious? It is good in a lot of ways! First of all, God's messages were spoken to the Jews. It is true that some Jews did not believe the message. **But does** this mean that God cannot be trusted, just because they did not have faith? **No indeed, God** tells the truth, even if everyone else is a liar. The scriptures says about God:

> *"Your words will be proven true,*
> *and in court You will win Your case"*

American, our evil deed show how right God is that what can we say? **Is it wrong** for God to become angry and punish us? What a foolish thing to ask. **But the answer is** "No." Otherwise, how could God judge the world? Since your lies bring great honor to God by showing how truthful He is, you may ask why God still says you are a sinner.

American, you might as well say; **Let's do** something evil, so that something good will come of it. Some people even claim that we are saying this. **But God** is fair and will judge them as well. **American why not say** - as we are being slanderously reported as saying one as some claim that we say - **Let us** do evil that good may result? Their condemnation is deserved. **Let God** be true and as it is written:

"So that you may be proved right in Your words and prevail in Your judging."

No One is Righteous

American, what does all this mean? Does it mean that we Jews are better off than the Gentiles? No, it doesn't! Jews as well as Gentiles are ruled by sins, just as I have said, American writings tell us:

*"**No one** is acceptable to God!*

Not one of them understands

or even searches for God.

They have turned away and are worthless.

There is not one person who does right.

Their words are like an open pit.

And their tongues are good only for telling lies.

Each word is as deadly as the fangs of a snake,

and they say nothing but bitter curses.

American, these people quickly become violent. Wherever they go, they leave ruin and destruction. **They** don't know how to live in peace. They don't even fear God?

American, we know that everything in the law was written for those who are under its power. **The law says** those things to stop anyone from making excuses and to let God accept people simply because they obey the law. No indeed! All the law does is to point out our sin.

American, I've been writing these hard things about us to show that we are all disobedient and that no one is excused. **When we come before God,** we have to admit the truth of all that I have written. **This makes us** feel very bad, because we know that its no good to blame God or others for the way we are. Each of us falls short of what God rightly expects of people made in His image.

God's Way of Accepting People

American, now we see how God does make us acceptable to him. The law and the prophets tell how we become acceptable and it isn't by obeying **the** law of Moses.

American, God treats everyone alike. He accepts people only because they have faith in **Jesus Christ. All of us have sinned and fallen short of God's glory. But God is** really kind and because of **Jesus Christ,** He freely accepts us and sets us free from our sins. **American, God sent Christ** to be our sacrifice. **Christ offered** His life's blood, so that by faith in Him we could come to God. **And God did** this to show that in the past He was right to be patient and forgive sinners. **This also** shows that God is right when He accepts people who have faith in **Jesus.**

American, what is left for us to brag about? Not a thing! It is because we obeyed some law? No! It is because of faith. **We see** that people are acceptable to God because they have faith and not because they obey what the law commands.

American, does God belong only to the Jews? Isn't He also the God of the Gentiles? Yes, He is! **There is only one God,** and He accepts Gentiles as well as Jews, simply because of their faith. **Do we** destroy the law by our faith? **Not at all!** We make it even more powerful. **Does this mean** that by faith we do away with the law? **Not at all!** Instead, we uphold the law.

American, Jesus Christ is the answer to the good news. **God has** provided the way of escape from the penalty of His law. **It's the way His Son Jesus** provided by paying our debt, by dying on the cross in our place. **There Jesus** accepted all of God's judgment for our sins. **When we receive Jesus** as our sinbearer, then God says we are "declared not guilty."

American, someone took your place, His name is Jesus Christ. Imagine you have committed a bad crime. You are in court and the judge is about to sentence you. **Then he stops** and calls someone from the back of the courtroom. It's the judge's own son. **He says you deserve to die for your crime, but my son has asked and I decided to let my very own son die for you. That is what Jesus did for you.**

American, does God destroy His law. NOT AT ALL! Through Jesus, God has made His law work better than ever. **Jesus carried** the load of our sins as He hung on the cross. Now God gives us, as a free gift, the goodness of **Jesus. He paid** all that we owed. **Now we** belong to God forever and we love to please the One who saved us.

Chapter 4
Abraham Justified by Faith

American, what can we say about our ancestor Abraham? **If he** became acceptable to God because of what he did, then he would have something to brag about to God. **The scriptures say, "God accepted Abraham because Abraham had faith in Him."**

American, money paid to workers isn't a gift. It is something they earn by working. **But you cannot** make God accept sinners only because they have faith in Him. **Scriptures say**, David talks about the blessings that come to people who are acceptable to God, even though they don't do anything to deserve these blessings.

American, when a man works, his wages are not credited to him as a gift but as an obligation. **However to the man** who does not work but trusts **God** who justifies the wicked, his faith is credited as righteousness. **David says** the same thing when he speaks of the blessedness of the man to whom God credits righteousness apart from works.

American, blessed are they whose transgressions are forgiven, whose sins are covered. **Blessed is the man** whose sin the Lord will never count against him.

American, David says, God Blesses people whose sins are forgiven and whose evil deeds are forgotten. **The Lord blesses** people whose sins are erased from His book.

American, is this blessedness only for the circumcised or also for the uncircumcised? We have been saying that Abraham's faith was credited to him as righteousness. Under what circumcision was it credited? Was it not after, but before! **American, he received** the sign of circumcision, a seal of the righteousness that he had by faith while he was still uncircumcised. So then he is the father of all who believe but have not been circumcised, in order that righteousness might be credited to them. **And he is also the father** of the circumcised who not only are circumcised but who also walk in the footsteps of the faith that our father Abraham had before he was circumcised.

American, you can't earn God's forgiveness. Abraham is an example of God's free gift. **We can't pay** to be saved, **but God himself** could bless us as a gift. **The gift** wasn't really free, **however Jesus paid**

the price with His own blood. Like Abraham we are accepted by God because of our faith.

American, King David knew about Jesus, sang in his Psalms about what Jesus would do. **He said that God** can wipe out our sins as though they never happened. Think about it - God is able to forget that we ever sinned against him. **Hospitals today often** circumcise baby boys, Jew and Gentile, for health reasons. In bible times, circumcision was for Jews only as a sign of membership in the family of God. But faith was the really important thing.

"Promise is for All who have Faith"

Believing without doubt in the word.

American, God promised Abraham and his descendants that he would give them the world. **This promise** was not made because Abraham had obeyed the law, but because his faith in God made him acceptable.

American, if Abraham and his descendants were given this promise because they had obeyed the law, then faith would mean nothing and the promise would be worthless.

American, God becomes angry when His law is broken. But where there isn't a law, it cannot be broken. **Everything depends** on having faith in God, so that God can help keep His promise because He is kind. **American, this promise** is not for Abraham's descendants who have the Law. **It is for all** who are Abraham's descendants because they have faith, just as he did. Abraham is the ancestor of us all. **American, the scriptures say** that Abraham would become the ancestor of many nations. **The promise was** made to Abraham because he had faith in God, who raises the dead to life and creates new things.

American, God promised Abraham a lot of descendants. And when it all seemed hopeless, **Abraham still had faith in God** and became the ancestor of many nations. **Abraham's faith never became weak**, not even when he was nearly a hundred years old. **He knew that** he was almost dead and that his wife Sarah could not have children. **American, Abraham never** doubted or questioned God's promise. His faith made him strong and he gave all the credit to God.

American, Abraham was certain that God could do what he had promised. So God accepted him, just as we read in the scriptures. They were written for us, **since we will also be accepted because of our faith in God, who raised our Lord Jesus Christ to life. God gave Christ to die for our sins, and He raised Him to life, so that we would be made acceptable to God.**

American, God promises eternal life to all believers, not only to Abraham and the Jews, but to all people. **God offers to save those who trust God as Abraham did. American, this promise is** as old as Abraham himself, because God promised him that his blessings would come to all nations. **American, that includes you and me.**

Chapter 5
What it Means to be Acceptable to God, Right with God and have Faith in Our Lord Jesus Christ

American, by faith we have been made acceptable to God. And now, because of our Lord Jesus Christ, we live at peace with God. **American, Christ has also** introduced us to God's kindness on which we take our stand. **So we are happy**, as we look forward to sharing in the glory of God. But that's not all! We gladly suffer because we know that suffering helps us to endure. And endurance builds character, which gives us a hope that will never disappoint us. **American, all of this happens** because God has given us the Holy Spirit, who fills our hearts with His love.

American, Christ died for us at a time when we were helpless and sinful. No one is really willing to die for an honest person, though someone might be willing to die for a truly good person. **American, God showed how much He loved us** by having Christ die for us, even though we were sinful.

American, there is more! Now that **God has accepted us because Christ sacrificed His life's blood,** we will also be kept safe from God's anger. **Even when we were God's enemies,** His Son died for us. Yet something even greater than friendship is ours. **Now that we are at peace with God,** we will be saved by His Son's life.

American, in addition to everything else, we are happy because God sent our Lord Jesus Christ to make peace with us.

American, God can be trusted, the first thing God wants us to do is have faith in Him. If we're sick and go to a doctor, but don't have faith in his or her ability, we might as well stay home. **Neither will God help us if we don't trust Him.**

American, the Holy Spirit helps us. At one time our future was uncertain but not any more. **Even though people may reject us,** we have the promise of God's friendship forever. **We know this because God's Holy Spirit now lives in us and assures us that God loves us.**

American, nothing separates us from God. Only our own refusal to accept His kindness can separate us from God. Imagine you have owed a lot of money to someone - so much you could never pay it. But then a rich friend pays off your debt for you. That is what Jesus did when He paid for your sins. So now you may be at peace with God.

Adam and Christ

Disobedient/Obedient

American, Adam sinned and that sin brought death into the world. Now everyone has sinned, and so everyone must die. Sin was in the world before the law came. **American, no record of sin was kept,** because there was no law. Yet death still had power over the time of Moses. **This happened,** though not everyone disobeyed a direct command from God, as Adam did. **American, from the time of Adam to the time Moses' death ruled over all mankind,** even over those who did not sin in the same way that Adam did when he disobeyed God's command.

American, in some ways Adam is like Christ who came later. But the gift that God was kind enough to give was very different from Adam's sin. That one sin brought death to many others. Yet in an even greater way, Jesus Christ alone brought God's gift

of kindness to many people. **American, God's grace**

is much greater and so is His free gift to so many

people through the grace of the one man, Jesus

Christ.

American, there is a lot of difference

between Adam's sin and God's gift. That one sin

led to punishment. **American, God's gift made it**

possible for us to be acceptable to Him, even though

we have sinned many times. Death ruled like a king

because Adam had sinned. That cannot compare with

what Jesus Christ has done. God has been so kind to

us and He has accepted us because of Jesus. And so we

will live and rule like kings. **American, how much**

greater is the result of what was done by the one

man, Jesus Christ. All who receive God's abundant

grace and are freely put right with Him will rule in

life through Christ.

American, everyone was going to be punished because Adam sinned. But because of the good things that Christ has done, God accepts us and gives us the gift of life. **American, Adam disobeyed God and caused many others to be sinners. Jesus obeyed God and will make many people acceptable to God. American, as all people were made sinners as the result of the disobedience of one man Adam, in the same way they will all be put right with God as the result of the obedience of the one man Jesus.**

American, the law came, so that full power of sin could be seen. Yet where sin was powerful, God's kindness was even more powerful. Sin ruled by means of death. **American, God's kindness now rules and God has accepted us because of Jesus Christ our Lord. This means that we will have eternal life. So American, just as sin ruled by means of death, so**

also God's grace rules by means of righteousness, leading us to eternal life through Jesus Christ our Lord.

American, we are sinful children of Adam, all children of our very first ancestor who passed on his sinful nature to us. Sin caused death. **American, God has made a way to help us.** Jesus undid the harm that Adam did by bringing sin into the world. By sending Jesus to die in our place God passed on Jesus' godly nature to all who accept Him.

American, what good did the law do? If God had not given us His law, we would not clearly know how great our disobedience is. That was the law's purpose - to show us our sins. We must not think that God gave us His law because we can be saved by keeping it. We can't. American, by His kindness God has given the gift of His Son, Jesus. When Jesus died and rose again from death, He made it possible for us to have our sins forgiven and to have life forever with

Him, Jesus.

Chapter 6
Dead in Sin but Alive because of Christ Having been Raised from Death to Life

American, what should we say? Should we keep on sinning, so that God's kindness will show up even better? **No American, we should not!** If we are dead to sin, how can we go on sinning? Don't you know that **all who share in Christ Jesus by being baptized** also share in His death? When we were baptized, we died and were buried with **Christ.** We were baptized, so that we would live a new life, as **Christ** was raised to life by **the glory of God the Father. America it is by our baptism,** that we were buried with Him and shared His death, in order that, just as Christ was raised from death by the glorious power of the Father, so also we might live a new life.

American, if we shared in Jesus' death by being baptized, we will surely be raised to life with Him. We know that the person we used to be was nailed to the cross with Jesus. **This was done,** so that our sinful bodies would no longer be the slaves of sin. We know that sin does not have power over dead people. For when a person dies, he is set free from the power of sin.

American, as surely as we died with Christ we believe we will also live with Him. We know that death no longer has any power over Christ. He died and was raised to life, never again to die. **American, when Christ died,** He died for sin once and for all.

But now He is alive and He lives only for God. In the same way, you must think of yourselves as dead to the power of sin. **But Christ Jesus has given life to you and you live for God.** So far as sin is concerned, but living in fellowship with God through Christ Jesus.

American, don't let sin rule your body. After all your body is bound to die, so don't obey its desires or let any part of it become a slave of evil. Give yourselves to God, as people who have been raised from death to life. **American, make every part of your body a slave that pleases God.** Don't let sin keep ruling your lives. You are ruled by God's kindness and not by the law. **Instead give yourselves to God,** as those who have been brought from death to life for righteous purposes. **Sin must not be your master;** for you do not live under the law but under God's grace.

American, what do we do about our sins? We should not go on sinning just because God has forgiven us. If God has forgiven us, we will hate our sins. **But we can't stop sinning by ourselves. If Christ lives** in us then we have a new life from Him because He rose from death. **But He also** put our sins to death when He died on the cross. **So we claim His** death as death for our sins. Our old selves are dead and we are now new people because Christ lives in us.

American, when we really put our faith in Christ, we feel so close to Him that it is as if we have experienced His death and new life. **We are dead to sin and alive with Christ. He helps us live in a new way - His way - a way that leaves no room for sins.**

American, God created our bodies very good. But since Adam's time, our bodies have become the means by which sin works. We live in physical bodies and our actions are carried out by our bodies. **But Christ's death for** us means that our bodies don't have to live for sin anymore.

Slaves Who Do What Pleases God

Slaves of Righteousness

American, what does all this mean? Does it mean we are free to sin, because we are ruled by God's kindness and not by the law? Certainly not! Don't you know that you are slaves of anyone you obey? You can be slaves of sin and die or you can be obedient slaves of God and be acceptable to Him.

American, you used to be slaves of sin. But I thank God that with all your heart you obeyed the teaching you received from me. Now you are set free from sin and are slaves who please God.

American, I am using these everyday examples, because in some ways you are still weak. You used to let the different parts of your body be slaves of your evil thoughts. **But now you must make**

every part of your body serve God, so that you will belong completely to Him.

American, when you were slaves of sin, you didn't have to please God. **But what good did you receive from** the things you did? All you have to show for them is your shame and they lead to death. Now you have been set free from sin and you are God's slaves. American, this make you holy and will lead you to eternal life. Sin pays off with death. But God's gift is eternal life given by Jesus Christ our Lord.

American, the law is not our master, when we live in sin, we live in fear, because the law reminds us of how sinful we are. But that fear caused by the law only makes us sin more and more. When God gives us the new life of Jesus, His Son, then we don't fear the law anymore. We want to obey God because we love Him, not because we're afraid.

American, we aren't free to sin! A criminal who has been in prison is set free. What does he do then? Does he go back to his old ways of crime? Not if he is smart. He has learned that crime doesn't pay. The Christian is like a criminal who has been set free by Christ. Now the Christian sees that obeying God is the true way of happiness and everlasting life. God's free gift is eternal life in union with Christ Jesus our Lord.

Chapter 7
An Illustration from Marriage

America, my friends, you surely understand enough about law to know that laws only have power over people who are alive. For example, the law says that a man's wife must remain his wife as long as he lives. But once her husband is dead, she is free to marry someone else. However, if she goes off with another man while her husband is still alive, she is said to be unfaithful.

American, that is how it is with you, my friends. You are now part of the body of Christ and are dead to the power of the law. You are free to belong to Christ, who was raised to life so that we could serve God. When we thought only of ourselves, the law made us have sinful desires. It made every part of our bodies into slaves who are doomed to die. For when we lived according to our human nature, the sinful desires stirred up by the law were at work in our bodies and we were useful in the service of death. But the law no longer rules over us. We are like dead people, and it cannot have any power over us. Now we can serve God in a new way by obeying His Spirit, and not in the old way by obeying the written law.

American, many marriages fail because people don't realize at the start that marriage is for life. I use marriage to show that we were once "married" to the law. But we died with Jesus when He died on the cross. Now we are free from the old law and we are "married" to Christ in His risen life. Marriage to Christ in this way is a happy marriage that lasts forever. Do you remember when someone told you when you were small, "Don't do that, or you'll be punished" but the command only made you want to do that thing even more? That is the way sin works through the law. Sin becomes worse because without being saved, sinners want to disobey what is right.

Law and Sin - The Battle with Sin

American, does this mean that the law is sinful? Certainly not! But if it had not been for the law, I would not have known what sin is really like. For example, I would not have known what it means to want something that belongs to someone else, unless the law had told me not to do that. It was sin that used this command as a way of making me have all kinds of desires. But without the law, sin is dead. Sin found its chance and by means of the commandment it deceived me and killed me.

American, before I knew about the law, I was alive. But as soon as I heard that command, sin came to life and I died. The very command that was supposed to bring life to me, instead brought death. Sin used this command to trick me, and because of it I died. Still the law and its commands are holy and correct and good. **American, am I writing** about the law that it may lead someone to think the law is an evil thing? Not so. Our sinful nature uses the law to make us sin worse. Until we receive Christ into our lives we continue to live in wickedness. When Jesus comes in, our love of sin passes away and we come to love goodness. Before Jesus becomes real to us as our Savior, our sins don't upset us very much. Then Jesus comes into our lives so our old slavery to sin and its misery can be broken. But if we don't ask Jesus for

His help, sin still tempts us and makes us unhappy. We can win when Jesus fights our war for us against sin.

Chapter 8
Life Through the Spirit: Living by the Power of Gods Spirit

American, if you belong to Christ Jesus, you won't be punished. The Holy Spirit will give you life that comes from Christ Jesus and will set you free from sin and death. The law of Moses cannot do this, because our selfish desires make the law weak. But God set you free when He sent His own Son to be like us sinners and to be a sacrifice for our sin. He did this so that we would do what the law commands by obeying the Spirit instead of our own desires.

American, people who are ruled by the desires think only of themselves. Everyone who is ruled by the Holy Spirit thinks about spiritual things. If our minds are ruled by our desires, we will die. But if our minds are ruled by the Spirit, we will have life and peace. Our desires fight against God, because they do not and cannot obey God's laws. If we follow our desires, we cannot please God.

American, you are no longer ruled by your desires, but by God's Spirit, who lives in you. People who don't have the Spirit of Christ in them don't belong to Him. But Christ lives in you. So you are alive because God has accepted you, even though your bodies must die because of your sins. Yet God raised Jesus to life! God's Spirit now lives in you, and He will raise you to life by His Spirit.

American, my dear friends, we must not live to satisfy our desires. If you do, you will die. But you will live by the help of God's Spirit you say "No" to your desires. Only those people who are led by God's Spirit. God's Spirit doesn't make us slaves who are afraid of Him. Instead we become His children and call Him our Father. God's Spirit makes us sure that we are His children. **American, His Spirit lets us know** that together with Christ we will be given what God has promised. We will also share in the glory of Christ, because we have suffered with Him. **The Spirit Himself** testifies with our spirit that we are God's children. Now if we are children, then we are heirs - heirs of God and co-heirs with Christ, if indeed we share in His sufferings in order that we may also share in His glory.

American, Jesus took our punishment, why did sin have to be punished? Why couldn't God just let everyone into heaven sins and all? But how would you like to live in a heaven where sinful people keep getting worse and worse forever and ever? That's why Jesus, the Son of God, let Himself be punished for our sins. Then God could take away our sins and let us live with Him forever. **American, when we are ruled by God's Spirit,** we love thoughts of God and goodness. This is a wonderful way to life, because we are then free from the desires that were killing us even when we didn't know they were.

American, Don't give in to all your desires. Think of the diseases and unhappiness that result from giving our bodies everything they want. We ought to feed our new spiritual nature on the things of the Holy Spirit. Then we will grow in our ability to love and enjoy God. This is exactly what we were created to do. **American, when a seed is planted,** it seems to die but it grows up into a beautiful new plant. When Jesus died for us, He was buried, but he rose again in a more wonderful body. Believers in Jesus will have wonderful bodies like His when they rise from death.

A Wonderful Future for God's People Future Glory

American, I am sure that what we are suffering now cannot compare with the glory that will be shown to us. In fact, all creation is eagerly waiting for God to show who His children are. Meanwhile, creation is confused, but not because it wants to be confused. American, God made it this way in the hope that creation would be set free from decay and would share in the glorious freedom of His children. We know that all creation is still groaning and is in pain, like a woman about to give birth. For we know that up to the present time all of creation groans with pain, like the pain of childbirth.

American, it is not just creation alone which groans; we who have the Spirit as the first of God's gifts also groan within ourselves as we wait for God to make us His sons and daughters and set our whole being free. The Spirit makes us sure about what we will be in the future. But now we groan silently, while we wait for God to show that we are His children. **American, this means that our bodies will also be set free.** And this hope is what saves us. But if we already have what we hope for, there is no need to keep on hoping. However, we hope for something we have not yet seen and we patiently wait for it. But if we hope for what we do not see, we wait for it with patience.

American, in certain ways we are weak, but the Spirit is here to help us. For example, when we don't know what to pray for, the Spirit prays for us in ways that cannot be put into words. All of our thoughts are known to God. He can understand what is in the mind of the Spirit, as the Spirit prays for God's people. **American, we know that God is always** at work for the good of everyone who loves Him. They are the ones God has chosen for His purpose and He has always known who His chosen ones would be. He had decided to let them become like His own Son, so that His Son would be the first of many children. God then accepted the people who have shared His glory would be with them. So those whom God set apart, He called and those He called, He put right with Himself and He shared His glory with them.

American, why does God's creation suffer? God has a plan to save His creation from the bad effects of sin. Now our world is full of decay, unhappiness and pain. But as a woman feels some pain when she is about to give birth to a baby, so too does the world feel pain now while it awaits the birth of a new and wonderful creation from God.

American, the Holy Spirit prays for us, we may sometimes pray for things that aren't really good for us, or we might not know what to pray for. But the Holy Spirit steps in and prays for us. The more and more we find ourselves praying for the things that will please God. And God is always arranging everything for our good - if we love Him.

American, God knows His children, here is a great mystery, but its not so strange if you think about it. God has always known who His people would be. He has been planning a whole new human race with Jesus as the head instead of Adam. Whoever wants to be in God's family can be a member by accepting Jesus.

God's Love in Christ Jesus

American, what can we say about all this? If God is on our side can anyone be against us? God did not keep back His own Son, but He gave Him for us. If God did this, won't He freely give us everything else? If God says His chosen ones are acceptable to Him, can anyone bring charges against them? **American,**

can anyone condemn them? No indeed! Christ died and was raised to life and now He is at God's side, speaking to Him for us. Can anything separate us from the love of Christ? Can trouble, suffering and hard times or hunger and nakedness or danger and death? It is exactly as the scripture says:

> *"For You we face death all day long.*
>
> *We are like sheep on their way to the butcher"*
>
> *"For Your sake we are in danger of death at all*
>
> *times;*
>
> *We are treated like sheep that are going to be*
>
> *slaughtered."*

American, in everything we have won more than a victory because of Christ who loves us. I am sure that nothing can separate us from God's love - not life or death, not angels or spirits, not the present or the future and not powers above or powers below.

Nothing in all creation can separate us from God's love for us in Christ Jesus our Lord!

American, is God on our side? Whether God is on our side depends on whether we are on God's side. If we are, nothing can stop us from doing and being all that God would like us to be. No one can accuse us or condemn us. God has accepted us. Nothing in heaven or earth or hell can separate us from Jesus. That's the greatest news in the world.

Chapter 9
God and His People

American, I am a follower of Christ, and the Holy Spirit is a witness to my conscience. So I tell the truth and I am not lying when I say my heart is broken and I am in great sorrow. I would gladly be placed under God's curse and be separated from Christ for the good of my own Jewish people. **American, they are the descendants of Israel**, and they are also God's chosen people. God showed them His glory. He made agreements with them and gave them His law. **American, the temple is theirs** and so are the promises that God made to them. They have those famous ancestors, who were also the ancestors of Jesus Christ. I pray that God, who rules over all, will be praised forever. Amen.

American, it cannot be said that God broke His promise. After all, not all of the people of Israel are true people of God. In fact when God made the promise to Abraham, He meant only Abraham's descendants by His son Isaac. God was talking only about Isaac when He promised Sarah, "At this time next year I will return and you will already have a son."

American, don't forget what happened to the twin sons of Isaac and Rebecca. Even before they were born or had done anything good or bad, the Lord told Rebecca that her older son would serve the younger one. **American, the Lord said** this to show that He makes His own choices and that it was not because of anything either of them had done. That's why the scriptures say that the Lord liked Jacob more than Esau.

American, are we saying that God is unfair? Certainly not! The Lord told Moses that He has pity and mercy on anyone He wants to. Everything then depends on God's mercy and not on what people want or do.

American, in the scriptures the Lord says to Pharaoh, I let you become king so that I could show you My power and be praised by all people on earth. Everything depends on what God decides to do, and He can either have pity on people or make them stubborn.

American, most people seem to be interested in themselves. That's why we are sometimes called the "me" generation. It comes as a shock to us to find a truly unselfish person. Paul loved his people more than himself. He said he would rather go to hell himself than see his people lost in sin. We should think about Paul's kind of love.

American, if God had been a human being, He would be unfair for choosing some and not others. He has mercy on some and not on others. But God is not a selfish man and He has perfect reasons for the decisions He makes, even if we can't understand His reasons. An infant doesn't understand it's parent either. But if we love God, we trust Him to do everything as it should be done.

God's Anger and Mercy

American, some one may ask, how can God blame us, if He makes us behave in the way He wants us to? But, my friend, I ask, "Who do you think you are to question God?" Does the clay have the right to ask the potter why he has shaped it the way he did?

Doesn't a potter have the right to make a fancy bowl and a plain out of the same lump of clay?

American, God wanted to show His anger and reveal His power against everyone who deserved to be destroyed. But instead, He patiently put up with them. He did this by showing how glorious He is when He has pity on the people He has chosen to share in His glory. American whether Jews or Gentiles, we are those chosen ones. **Just as the Lord says in the book of Hosea:**

> *"Although they are not My people,*
>
> *I will make them My people.*
>
> *I will treat with love those nations*
>
> *that have never been loved."*

Once they were told, "You are not My people.. But in that very place they will be called children of the living God."

American, this is what the prophet Isaiah said about the people of Israel;

> *"The people are as many as the*
>
> *grains of sand along the beach."*

But only a few who are left will be saved. American, the Lord will be quick and sure to do on earth what He has warned He will do.

American, also it is written, "If the Lord All Powerful had not spared some of our descendants, we would have been destroyed like the cities of Sodom and Gomorrah." **God's mercy was the reason** He chose to save some. He could have let us all go to hell, but in His kindness He decided to send His Son to die for people. Then whoever really wanted to could be saved by choosing Christ. Which are you choosing today; your own way or God's way? That choice tells the story of your future.

Israel and The Good News "Gospel"

American, what does this mean? It means that the Gentiles were not trying to be acceptable to God, but they had faith. It also means that the people were not acceptable to God. And why not?

American, it was because they were trying to be acceptable by obeying the law instead of by having faith in God. The people of Israel fell over the stone that makes people stumble, **just as God says in the scriptures;**

> *"Look! I am placing in Zion a stone to*
>
> *make people stumble and fall.*

But those who have faith in that one will never be disappointed."

American, my friends, how I wish with all my heart that my own people might be saved! How I pray to God for them! I can assure you they are deeply devoted to God; but their devotion is not based on the true knowledge. They have not known the way in which God puts people right with himself and instead, they have tried to set up their own way; and so they did not submit themselves to God's way of putting people right. For Christ has brought the law to an end, so that everyone who believes is put right with God.

American, God opened a way for all to be saved, by faith. He also put a stone in front of those who would try to earn their way into heaven. All without faith would stumble over that stone, which is Jesus.

The law is for knowing what God expects, but it can't make people good. The law helps people realize they are sinners. Trying to be accepted by keeping the law is a "dead-end street.' God accepted people by faith in His Son Jesus.

Chapter 10
Salvation is for All

American, the scriptures say that a person could become acceptable to God by obeying the law. He did this when He wrote, "If you want to live, you must do all that the law commands."

But people whose faith makes them acceptable to God will never ask, "Who will go up to heaven to bring Christ down?" Neither will they ask, "Who will go down into the world of the dead to raise Him to life?"

American, all who are acceptable because of their faith simply say, "The message is as near as your mouth or your heart." And this is the same message we preach about faith.

American, you will be saved if you say that God raised Jesus Christ from death and if you believe this with all your heart. God will accept you and save you, if you truly believe this and tell it to others!

American, scriptures say that no one who has faith will be disappointed no matter if that person is a Jew or a Gentile, all mankind. There is only one Lord and He is generous to everyone who asks for His help. All who call out to the Lord will be saved.

American, but how can people ask the Lord to save them if they have never had faith in Him? How can they hear about Him unless someone tells them? And how can anyone tell them without being sent by the Lord? **The scriptures say** it is a beautiful sight to see even the feet of someone coming to preach the good news. Yet not everyone has believed the message.

American, no one has faith without hearing the message about Christ. But I ask, "Is it true that they did not hear the message?" Of course they did - for as the scripture says:

"The sound of their voice went out to all the world;

their words reached the ends of the earth.."

Did the people not understand? **The scriptures say** that the Lord has said, **"The message was told everywhere on earth. It was announced all over the world."**

American, did the people not understand? Moses himself told that the Lord has said,

"I will make My people jealous; who

are a so-called nation of nobodies.

I will make them angry at people who

don't understand a thing."

And Isaiah is even bolder when he says,

"I was found by those who were not looking for me."

American, but concerning Israel He says, "All day long I held out my hand to welcome a disobedient and rebellious people."

American, anyone can be saved, by our faith in Jesus. God accepts people by faith in His Son Jesus. The law is for knowing what God expects, but it can't make people good. The law helps people realize they are sinners. Trying to be accepted by keeping the law is a "dead-end street."

American, do you want to be saved? You don't have to know everything the Christian experts know. You only have to know that God is waiting for you to come back to Him. Everyone is saved who asks God for forgiveness because of Jesus who died and rose again. By faith in your heart truly believe this and tell it to others.

The Lord is looking for someone to truly tell the Good News about His Son Jesus Christ. God wants us to carry this good news about how to be saved in truth all over the world and many are doing this. The nations can't believe in Jesus if we don't be truthful and tell the truth.

The good news comes to the Gentiles. The Jews heard the good news first, but many of them refused to put their faith in Jesus. So God continued with His plan. He used some of the Jewish believers to carry the good news to the people of other nations, and a great many of them trusted in Christ as their Savior.

American, in the scriptures the Lord says to His people,

> *"All day long Jesus Christ has reached*
> *out His hand to welcome*
> *the people who are stubborn and refuse to obey."*

Chapter 11
God Has Not Rejected His People

American, am I saying that God has turned His back on His people? **Certainly not!** God did not turn His back on His chosen people. Don't you remember reading in the scriptures how Elijah complained to God about the people of Israel? **He said, "Lord, they killed your prophets and destroyed your altars. I am the only one left and now they want to kill me."**

American, but the Lord told Elijah, "I still have seven thousand followers who have not worshipped Baal." **It is the same way now. God was**

kind to the people of America and so a few of them are still His followers. This happened because of God's kindness and not because of anything they have done. It could not have happened except for God's kindness.

American, this means that only a few of the people of America found what all of them were searching for. And the rest of them were stubborn, just as the scriptures say,

> *"God made them so stupid that their eyes are blind*
>
> *and*
>
> *their ears are still deaf."*

Then said,

> *"Turn their meals into bait for a trap*
>
> *so that they will stumble*
>
> *and be given what they deserve.*
>
> *Blindfold their eyes! Don't let them see,*
>
> *Bend their backs beneath a burden that will never be*
>
> *lifted."*

American, as the scripture says, "God made their minds and hearts dull; to this very day they cannot see or hear."

"May they be caught and trapped at their feasts,

may they fall, may they be punished?

May their eyes be blinded so that they cannot see;

and make them bend under their troubles at all

times."

A.   Gentiles Will Be Saved

American, do I mean that the Jewish people fell, never to get up again? Certainly not! Their failure made it possible for the American to be saved and this will make the Jewish people jealous. But if the rest of the world's people were helped so much by Jew's sin and loss, they will be helped even more by Jew's full return.

I am now speaking to you American, and as long as I am an apostle to you, I will take pride in my work. I hope in this way to make some of my own people jealous enough to be saved. When Jews rejected God, the rest of the people on the world were able to turn to Him. So when God makes friends with America, it will be like bringing the dead back to life.

American, part of a batch of dough is made holy by being offered to God, then all of the dough is holy. If the roots of a tree are holy, the rest of the tree is holy too!

American, we are like branches of a wild olive tree that were made to be part of a cultivated olive tree. You have taken the place of some branches that were cut away from it. And because of this, you enjoy the blessing that comes from being part of that cultivated tree. **American, don't think** you are better than the branches that were cut away. Just remember that you are not supporting the roots of that tree. Its roots are supporting you.

American, maybe you think those branches were cut away, so that you could be put in their place. That's true enough. But they were cut away because they did not have faith, and you are where you are because you do have faith. So don't be proud, but be afraid. **If God cut away those natural branches, couldn't He do the same to you?**

American, now you see both how kind and how hard God can be. He was hard on those who fell, but He was kind to you. And he will keep on being kind to you, if you keep on trusting in His kindness. Otherwise you will be cut away too.

American, if those other branches will start having faith, they will be made a part of that tree again. God has the power to put them back. **American, after all,** it was not natural for branches to be cut from a wild olive tree and to be made part of a cultivated olive tree. **So it is much more likely that God will join the**

natural branches back to the cultivated olive tree and couldn't He do the same to you? American, we can't be proud about being Christians. All that we are and have comes from God. We are like branches in a tree. Not only that, but we're like small branches in a bigger tree that God has planted. Abraham, the father of the Jews, was the original root of the tree. The early branches were the Jews. American, believers are branches that are put onto God's tree.

B.   God's Mercy on All

American, there is a secret truth, my friends, I don't want you Americans to be too proud of yourselves. So I will explain the mystery of what has happened to the people of Abraham's ancestors. Some of them have become stubborn and they will stay like that until the complete number of you Americans have come.

In this way all Americans will be saved, as the scriptures say,

"From Zion some will come to rescue us. Then Abraham's descendants will stop being evil and remove all wickedness."

This is what the Lord has promised to do when He forgives their sins. I will make this covenant with them when I take away their sins.

American, the people are treated as God's enemies, so that the good news can come to you. But they are still the chosen ones and God loves them because of their famous ancestors. God does not take back the gifts He has given or forget about the people He has chosen.

But now America has rejected God, and you have been shown mercy. And because of the mercy shown to you, they will also be shown mercy. All people have disobeyed God, and that's why He treats them as prisoners. **But God does this,** so that He can have mercy on all of them.

Who can measure the wealth and wisdom and knowledge of God? Who can understand His decisions or explain what He does?

"Has anyone known the thoughts of the Lord or given Him advice? Has anyone loaned something to the Lord that must be repaid?"

American, everything comes from the Lord. All things were made because of Him and will return to Him. Praise the Lord forever! Amen.

American, how great are God's riches? How deep are His wisdom and knowledge? Who can explain His decisions? Who can understand His ways? We can't figure out God's ways. Our goal in life is to obey Jesus, not to understand all that He is doing. We know that He does everything right and He does everything well. God is the Creator and Owner of all that we can and cannot see. America, all that we have came from Jesus our Lord and Savior. We just have to trust Jesus for the things we can't understand.

Chapter **12**
Life in God's Service

American, God is good. So, my friends, I beg you to offer yourselves as a living sacrifice to God pure and pleasing to Him. This is the true worship that you should offer.

Since God owns everything anyway, you can't give Him anything He doesn't already possess. But you can willingly give back your life to Him as an act of thanksgiving. Jesus died for you, so surely you can live for Him. Then let Jesus change your mind.

When you think Jesus thoughts your life will be happy. Because you are happy, you will then want to please God.

American, I realize how kind God has been to me, and so I tell each of you not to think you are better than you really are. Use good sense and measure yourself by the amount of faith God has given you. Just as the body has many parts in one body and all the parts do not have the same function. That's how it is with us there are many of us, but we are one body in Christ.

God has also given each of us different gifts to use. If our gift is to speak the good news of God's message, we should do it according to the faith that we have. God has given us different jobs to do. We honor God and we reach our goals by doing well whatever He gives us to do in the world. **What do you think God wants you to do for Him?**

American, do your job in obedience to God by faith, if we can serve, we should serve; if it is to teach, we should teach; if it is to encourage others, we should do so. If we can give, we should be generous. If we are leaders, we should do our best with wisdom and knowledge of God's teaching. If we share kindness to others, we should do it cheerfully.

A.   Christian Living

American, be sincere in your love for others. Hate what is evil, hold on to what is good. Love one another warmly as Christian brother and sisters and honor others more than you do yourself. If we have the love of God in our hearts, then we will do all things in a way that pleases Him. We can't do wrong to anyone if we are controlled by love of God. And we should have a special love for other believers, our brothers and sisters in the Lord. Work hard, serve the Lord and eagerly follow the Holy Spirit.

Let your hope keep you joyful. Be patient in your time of trouble and never stop praying. Hope looks for the best even when things are going wrong. And hope comes from having a healthy trust in God. We don't always understand what God plans to do, but we know He does everything just as it should be done. Then we are glad and have hope. Share your belongings by taking care of Christian needy people and welcome strangers into your home.

American, ask God to bless everyone who mistreats you. Yes, ask Him to bless them and not to curse them. Be happy with those who are happy. Have the same friendliness with everyone. Don't be proud, make friends with humble people. Do not be wise in your own estimations.

If someone has done you wrong, do not repay him with a wrong. But try to earn the respect of others and do everything possible on your part to live in peace with everybody. My friends, don't try to get even. Let God take revenge.

American, the Lord says, "I am the one to take revenge and pay back" Also I say, "If your enemies are hungry, give them something to eat. And if they are thirsty, give them something to drink. This will be the same as pouring burning coals on their heads." This will make him burn with shame.

You can't trust those who do you wrong, but hating them isn't the answer either. Feelings of hate destroy the hater more than the hated person. People who have a hateful spirit are actually ruining their health and taking years off their lives. It's better to be kind to our enemies as God was kind to us. Do not let evil defeat you, instead, conquer evil with good.

Chapter 13
Obey Authority

American, my brothers, because of God's great love to us, I appeal to you; everyone must obey state authorities, because no authority exists without God's permission, and those opposing authorities have been put there by God. People who ever oppose the authorities are opposing what God has done and anyone who does so will bring judgment on himself. For rulers are a threat to evil people not to good people. There is no need to be afraid of the authorities. Just do right and they will praise you for it. After all, they are God's servants for your own good and help you.

American, if you do wrong, you ought to be afraid, because these rulers have the right to punish you. They are God's servants who punish criminals and carry out God's punishment on those who do wrong. For this reason people must obey the authorities - not just because of God's punishment, but also as a matter of conscience.

American, you must also pay your taxes, because the authorities are working for God's servants when they fulfill their duties and it is their duty to take care of these matters. Pay them what you owe them, pay them your personal and property taxes and show respect and honor for them all.

American, we shouldn't imagine that because we're Christians we don't have to obey laws. Some people in history have imagined that and they have done a lot of harm to God's work in the world. Of course we can't obey laws that really cause us to disobey God. But in general Christians are good citizens who pay their taxes and do what the law says.

American, rulers may not always mean to serve God, but God sees to it that they do. They carry out God's plan whether they wish to or not. So you don't need to be afraid of authorities, even cruel ones. God will take care of us just the same.

A.   Love one Another

American, be obligated to no one! If people love one another, they've done all that the laws of God demand. The commandments such as be faithful in marriage, **do not murder, do not steal and do not want what belongs to others** are summed up in one command that says, "Love your neighbor as you love yourself." If you love someone, you will never do him harm or wrong. So to love one another is to obey all that the law of God demands.

American, Jesus summed up the law of God by commanding us to love another. I say when we love others we do them no wrong. But we do them alot of good. The good news about Jesus would spread all over the world if Christians loved one another completely.

B.   When Christ Returns

American, you must do this, in the time you are

living and so you should live properly. It is time to awake from sleep. Our salvation is nearer now than when we put our faith in the Lord. Night is almost over and the day is at hand. We must stop behaving as people do in the dark and put on the armor of light so you can live in the light of the Lord. **Let**

us conduct ourselves properly not as people do today. Don't waddle in carousing and drunkenness, in sexual promiscuity and sensuality, not in fighting or jealousy, **but put on the Lord Jesus Christ** and make no provision for the flesh in regard to its lusts. Then you won't try to satisfy your selfish desires.

American, Jesus is coming soon, we live in the days and time where America is so evil and that it seemed the Lord must come very soon. This world is passing away. Since we know the Lord is surely coming, we should spend our lives in ways that honor Christ and bless others.

Chapter **14**
Do Not Judge Your Brother

American, accept the person who, is weak in faith, but not for the purpose of passing judgment on his opinions. One man has faith that he may eat all things but he who is weak eats vegetables only. **Let not the person** who eats despise with contempt him who does not eat and let not him who does not eat, judge him who eats for God has accepted him. Who are you to judge the servant of another? It is only their Lord who is able to decide whether he succeeds or fails. The Lord will make sure that they do right.

American, some person of the Lord's followers think one day is more important than another. Each one should be fully convinced in his own mind. Some person thinks highly of special day, does so in honor of the Lord. Some person will eat anything, does so in honor of the Lord and he gives thanks to God.

American, whether a person lives or dies, it must be for God rather than for ourselves. If we live, we live to the Lord and if we die, we die to the Lord. So whether a person lives or dies we belong to the Lord. For Christ died and rose to life in order to be the Lord of the living and of the dead. You, then, why do you judge your brother? Why do you look down on your brother? For we will all stand before God's judgment seat.

American, it is written, "As surely as I live, says the Lord, every knee will bow before me, every tongue confess to God." So then, each person will give an account of himself to God. It's important to know why we live. We quickly come to the end of our earthly lives and we shouldn't waste, the time God has given us. We won't get to live this life again. We want to be able to say, "I spent my time trying to honor God."

American, we may have to judge others abilities to decide what they are fit to do, but we can't decide what God thinks about people. He is the only judge of that. We may be surprised to find out that same people we turn away from now are people God will one day accept.

A.   Do Not Make Your Brother Fall

American, therefore let us stop passing judgment on one another. Instead, make up your mind not to put any stumbling block or obstacle in your brothers way. As one who is in the Lord Jesus, I am fully convinced that no food is unclean in itself.

But if anyone believes that some food is unclean, then it is unclean for him. If you hurt your brother because of something you eat, then you are no longer acting from love. **Do not let** the food that you eat destroy the person for whom Christ died! **Do not let** what you consider good to be spoken of as evil.

American, God's kingdom is not a matter of eating and drinking, but of the righteousness, peace and joy which the Holy Spirit gives. When someone serves Christ in this way it is pleasing to God and is approved by others.

So then, we must always try to live at peace and help each other have a strong faith. **Do not** destroy the work of God for the sake of food. All food is clean. All food may be eaten but it is wrong for a person to eat anything that causes someone to stumble. **It is better not** to eat meat or drink wine or to do anything else that will cause your brother to stumble or fall.

American, whatever you believe about these things keep between yourself and God. Blessed is the man who does not condemn himself by what he approves. But if you have doubts about what you eat, God condemns you when you eat it because your action is not based on faith. And you know that it is wrong because anything you do against your faith is sin.

Chapter 15
Please Others Not Yourself

American, if our faith is strong we should be

patient with the Lord's followers whose faith is weak.

Each of us should please his neighbor for his good,

to build him up. For Christ did not please himself.

Instead, as it is written, "The insults of those who

insult you have fallen on me." Everything was written

to teach us, in order that we might have hope through

the patience and encouragement which the scriptures

give us.

American, may God the one who makes us patient and cheerful give you a spirit of unity among yourselves as you follow Christ Jesus.

A.   The Good News is for Jews and Gentiles

American, honor God by accepting each other as Christ has accepted you in order to bring praise to God. For I tell you that Christ's life of service was on behalf of the Jews, to show that God is faithful to make His promises to their ancestors come true. So that the Gentiles may glorify God for His mercy as it is written,

"I will tell the nations about you and I will sing

hymns to Your name"

American, again it says,

"Rejoice O Gentiles, with His people"

American, again it says,

"Praise the Lord all you Gentiles

and sing praises to Him all you peoples."

American, again, Isaiah says,

"Someone from David's family will come to power.

One who will arise to rule over the nations,

the Gentiles will put their hope in Him."

American, I pray that God, the source of hope, fill you with all joy and peace by means of your faith in Him, so that your hope will continue to grow by the power of the Holy Spirit.

B.   Work as a Missionary

American, I myself am convinced, my friends, I am sure that you are very good and that you have all the knowledge you need to teach each other. I have written you quite boldly on some points, as if to remind you of them again, because of the grace God gave me to be a minister of Christ Jesus to the Gentiles with the priestly duty of proclaiming the gospel of God, so that the Gentiles might become an offering acceptable to God, sanctified by the Holy Spirit.

American, because of Christ Jesus, then I can be proud of my service for God. I will be bold and write only about what Christ has done through me to lead the Gentiles to obey God. He has done this by means of words and deeds, by the power of miracles and wonders and by the powers of the Spirit of God. My ambition has always been to proclaim the Good News in places where Christ has not been heard of so as not to build on a foundation laid by someone else.

American, it is written, those who were not told about Him will see and those who have not heard will understand.

Plan For America

American, I have been prevented many times from writing so boldly to you. For years I have wanted to write this letter to a church that existed before I made the journey that we read about at the end of the book of Acts. It may be that the American church was started by Roman Jews who were present at the Day of Pentecost told about in Acts.

American, I urge you, brothers by our Lord Jesus Christ and by the love that the Spirit gives; join me in praying fervently to God for me. Pray that I may be kept safe from the unbelievers of the American people and that my service in America may be acceptable to God's people. And so that by God's will I may come to you with joy and together with you be refreshed. The God of peace be with you all.

American, I urge you to watch out for those who cause division and put trouble in your way those that are contrary to the teaching you have learned in this writing by the power of the Holy Spirit for we will all stand before God's judgment seat and each of us will give an account of himself to God. Watch out for troublemakers, keep away from them. For such people are not serving our Lord Christ, but their own appetites. By smooth talk and flattery they deceive the minds of naive people. Everyone has heard about your obedience, so I am full of joy over you, but want you to be wise about what is good and innocent, about what is evil. The grace of our Lord Jesus be with you.

Chapter 16
Solid Foundation Live to Please God

American, Living to please God may seem like a daunting task. And for some, nit is. They struggle to live up to a list of do's and don'ts. They try to obtain God's favor through acts of kindness and compassion. They attempt to "appease" God for their sinful behavior by going to church or making a "confession." But this passage – in fact, this entire chapter in America – lets you know that it is possible to live a life that is pure and pleasing to God.

American, The beginning verses of this chapter explain that once we enter into a relationship with Jesus Christ, God frees us from the "vicious circle" of sin and death through the power of his Holy Spirit. This terminology illustrates the basis of our freedom: in essence, the Holy Spirit you received by accepting Jesus Christ into your life has made you a "slave" of Jesus Christ – not a "slave" of your sinful nature.

American, The apostle C. Leo often identified himself as a slave of Jesus Christ in his writings. He used the word "duolos" or "bondslave," was a slave who had been granted freedom by his master, but who loved his master so deeply that he voluntarily chose to continue on as that master's servant. Likewise, C. Leo was not a slave to Christ because he had to be; he was a slave to Christ because he wanted to be. He had totally surrendered himself to his Master.

American, The only way to be free from sin is to be "bound" to Jesus. Unless you completely surrender your life to the Lord, all of your efforts to lead a pure life will be futile. That old sinful nature will continue to rear its ugly head and influence your thoughts and actions. But if you are a bondslave of Jesus, following the leading of the Holy Spirit (verse 5), you will not serve God out of fear and duty but out of love and gratitude. Your service will not be motivated by a desired to earn God's approval but will be motivated by a desire to be close to Jesus, recognizing that you already have that approval because of what Jesus did for you. This "blessed" bondage gives you the will, the power, and the motivation to live a life that is pleasing to God.

Our Lives Should Show That God

Is at Work in Our Hearts

While we still live on this side of heaven, we will always struggle between the desire to obey God and the desire to follow our sinful instincts. Even the apostle C. Leo knew that it was like to struggle with sin. In the verses surrounding this text, he describes the six keys to winning this battle and living a life that not only pleases God, but shows that God is working in our heart.

1. **American,** Admit the Power of Sin in Your Life (see Romans 7:14). Recognize that you have that "combustible nature" within you, a vulnerability to the enticements of sin. If we fail to see our potential weakness, we are even more vulnerable to fall to them. The Bible warns against such an attitude, saying, "If you think you are standing strong, be careful, for

you too many fall into the same sin" (1 Corinthians 10:12).

2. **American,** Realize That You Are Powerless to Change on Your Own (see Romans 7:18). Your sinful nature is the source of the problem. You will never "master" sin and live a life pleasing to God on your own. Apart from God, you can do nothing.

3. **American,** Become "Fed Up" with Your Condition and Cry for Help (see Romans 7:24). You cannot control evil in your life by simply determining to do so. You have to come to the end of yourself and ask for God's help in this struggle.

4. **American,** Accept Your Freedom (see Romans 7:25). Take the hand of help that is offered to you by Jesus.

5. **American,** Accept God's Forgiveness and lack of Condemnation (see Romans 8:12). Because of your unique union with Christ, God will forgive you

– not condemn you – when you acknowledge your failures, struggles, and broken commitments.

6. **American,** Cut the Instinctive Actions of Your Sinful Nature (see Romans 8:3-8). The only way to stop committing instinctive sinful action is to stop living by your sinful nature and start living by the power of the Holy Spirit. How do you do this? As verse 6 implies, you must relinquish control of your mind to the Spirit. When you do this, you will be "controlled by the Holy Spirit {and } think about things that please the spirit" (Romans 8:5).

You will always have the potential to sin. But God has given you the power to overcome sin through his Holy Spirit. The key to drawing on his power is to obedient to the Holy Spirit.

Our Peace Continues As We Follow the Holy Spirit ROMANS 8:5-8

American, Even if you are a Christian, you still must struggle with your sinful nature. However, if you allow God's Holy Spirit to control your life, that struggle will be much less intense. For, as this passage says, you will want to live to please God.

American, If you follow your old evil desires, you "can never please God" (verse 8). Your life – whether you realize it or not – will be empty. But if you live the Spirit – controlled life, you will experience "life and peace" (verse 6). To enter into the Spirit – controlled life, follow the advice of the apostle Paul, "Let heaven fill your thoughts. Do not think only about things down here on earth. For you died when Christ died, and your real life is hidden with Christ in God" (Colossians 3:2-3).

Knowing Whom You Belong to and What the Future Holds Brings True Joy

This verse touches upon three important facets of the Christians life that should give you great joy:

1. **American,** You Have a New Identity. When you accept Jesus Christ into your life, God gives you a new identity. You discover that you are not merely some product of random chance. You are not a speck in the universe. You are a child of God. And as God's child you can rest assured that you will be loved and cared for by your heavenly Father.

2. **American,** You Have Power to Face Life. America, with that new identity and hope in Christ, you also have the promise of the Holy Spirit's presence and power in your life. The Holy Spirit works constantly in your heart, helping you to understand God's Word and to transform your attitudes and behavior. An expanded

translation of this verse says that by the power of the Holy Spirit, your whole life and outlook will be "radiant with hope." God has not left you to face life on your own. He has promised to guide and strengthen you with this Spirit.

3. **American,** You Have Hope for the Future. America, As a Christian, you have the hope and knowledge that there is life beyond the grave. Your last breathe on earth will be followed by your first breathe in heaven. We know this is true, because God has promised it in his Word. This verse asserts that your belief in Jesus and his promises to us as his followers will fill you with joy and peace.

The world offers many roads to happiness: sex, money, power, personal success. But they are all cheap and worthless substitues in comparison to knowing that you are God's child and that you have the hope of heaven. This is the only road to lasting – indeed,

eternal – joy.

Chapter 17
Big Questions

What Happens to Those Who Have Never Heard the Gospel? Read Romans 1:18-20

American, Sometimes the person who asks this question is not so much concerned about those who have never heard the gospel. Rather, this person may be more concerned about trying to put up a "smoke screen" to keep you – the Christian – from showing his or her need for God. We might remind that person that God is loving and compassionate, and that he will deal fairly and justly with those who have never heard the gospel. But the person who asks you this question needs to recognize that knowledge brings responsibility. Those who know the truth of the gospel will be held accountable.

American, As we know from the Bible, God will judge us according to what we know of him (see Luke 12:48). We will not be held accountable for what we do not know. Still, that does not excuse us from all responsibility. Otherwise we might say "Ignorance is bliss." But this is not to say that the person who has not heard of Jesus will never know of him.

American, We, as human, no matter where we live on God's earth, were born with a soul, an emptiness, a sense that life should have meaning and purpose. In spite of that spiritual longing, we have disregarded God and his Word. But if we are truly seeking God, he will reveal himself to us. We find proof of this in Acts

10:1-48. There, a man named Cornelius – a religious man who constantly prayed to God – asked the Lord to reveal himself to him. Although Cornelius may have heard of Jesus Christ, he did not know God's plan for salvation. But that did not stop God from answering his prayer by sending the apostle Peter to preach the gospel to him. When Cornelius heard that wonderful message, he believed! The Bible tells us that God is unchanging (see James 1:17). He is the same yesterday, today, and tomorrow. If he heard Cornelius's prayer, he will also hear the prayers of those who do not know him but desire to.

If God is So Good, Why Do Bad Things Happen to His People?

American, Sickned, war, accident, natural disasters, tragedies – they come to the just and the unjust, the Christian and the non-Christian, the moral and the immoral. Yet, if God is so good and all powerful, why doesn't he just wipe out evil things in this world? This question often arises after any tragedy, but especially when it affects people who you would think should be "immune" to such things.

American, In addressing this question, it is important to remember that God originally created the world perfect. But he also gave man the freedom to obey or to disobey. When Adam sinned, death and suffering became an inevitable part of life (verse 12). Yet, as the Christian thinker C.S. Lewis observed, it is idle for us to speculate about the origin of evil. The problem we all face is the fact of evil. The only solution to the fact of evil is God's solution, Jesus Christ (Paul Little, How to Give Away Your Faith (Downers Grove, III.: InterVarsity Press, 1966).

American, How is Jesus Christ the solution to the fact of evil? The moment you surrendered your life to Jesus Christ, you entered into the master plan that God has for you. Though it is true that you may not know what the future holds, you know who holds the future. And he has promised that all things work together for good to those that love God (see Romans 8:28). Not just the good things, but all things.

American, That is easy to say when things are going smoothly. But when something unexpected comes into the picture we may wonder if God is paying attention. That is when we need to realize that God is painting on a large canvas. He is looking at the big picture. We only see what is in front of us at the given moment.

American, God will allow many events to come into our life – good things, bad things, things that make sense, things that make no sense at all. But every one of these incidents in our lives serves as a part of his plan for us. Tragedy in itself is not good. But God can take tragedy and hardship and use them for his glory. As God's children, we know that everything that happens to us first goes through his screen of protection. And he will never give us more than we can handle (see 1 Corinthian 10:13). For that reason we can follow the advice in verse 3 and rejoice. We have the assurance that God is working in our lives to strengthen and develop our character. More important, he will never leave our side (see Hebrews 13:5).

How Should I View Authority? Read ROMANS 13:1-2

American, When dealing with the subject of authority – particularly how one should act toward those in the government – the Bible gives us some important things to consider.

American, god Raises Up Rulers. It is true that not every government official has been obedient to God. In fact, far too many have directly violated his Word. Yet God has allowed certain people to rule for his purposes. In the Old Testament God often allowed certain "evil" countries to come to power in order to punish Israel for their wrongdoing and to remind them of their need to return to God. Therefore, we need to respect those in authority, since God has divinely appointed them.

American, God Uses Those in Government Who Fear Him. While God is ultimately in control of every event that takes place in the world, he still uses his people in strategic position of power. When Queen Esther, a Jew, faced the prospect of seeing her people put to death, her Uncle Mordecai challenged her with these words: "If you keep quiet at a time like this, deliverance for the Jews will arise from some other place, but you and your relatives will die. What's more, who can say but that you have been elevated to the palace for just such a time as this " (Esther 4:14)? Certainly, God does not forbid us to be part of the political process.

Sometimes he will even use Christians in government to accomplish his purposes.

American, We are to Be a Witness to Those in Authority. Your obedience to the laws of the land serves as a witness to the God you serve. Peter, addressing the early Christians who were suffering persecution under the cruel tyranny of Nero, still challenged believers to be law abiding citizens (see peter 2:13-15).

American, Our Allegiance to God Should Always Come First. What about those times when a law or government does something that directly contradicts God's law? We are accountable to a higher authority. In the Old Testament we read how Daniel defied the king's decree that forbade people to pray to anyone but him (Daniel 6:1-28). Daniel knew that God had said to worship him alone, so he obeyed God's law instead of man's. As you may recall, he was sent to the lion's den, but God spared is life by shutting the lion's mouths. In the New Testament, peter told the high priest, when he had been warned not to talk about Jesus, "we must obey God rather than human authority" (Acts 5:29). In more recnt times, Christians in Communist and Muslim countries continue to share Christ and distribute Bibles, despite laws that make such actions illegal.

American, Perhaps the best approach to those in authority over us is to follow the advice found in 1 Peter 2: 17: "Fear God. Show respect for the king." Here we see a perfect balance, for as we fear God in our daily lives, we will live above reproach and be examples to those in authority. At the same time, we will be able to discern when humans laws contradict the divine laws established by God.

My Closing Prayer

Praise God, Let us give glory to God! He is able to make you stand firm in your faith, according to the Good News. I preach about Jesus Christ and according to the revelation of the secret truth, which was hidden for long ages in the past. Now, however, that truth has been brought out into the open through the writings of the prophets; and by the command of the eternal God it is made known to all nations so that all may believe and obey!

O God, the Father of our Lord Jesus Christ, when we pray for you. For we have heard of your faith in Christ Jesus and of your love for all God's people. When the true message, the Good News first came to you, you heard about the hope it offers. So your faith and love are based on what you hope for which is kept safe for you in heaven. The gospel keeps bringing blessings and is spreading throughout the world, just as it has among you ever since the day you first heard about the grace of God and came to know it as it really is. You learned of God's grace for America, our dear fellow servant, **who** is Christ's faithful worker on our behalf! He has told us of the love that the Holy Spirit has given you. In the name of Jesus.

The Way to New Life

Six Scriptural Steps to Salvation

Men still cry, "What must I do to be saved?" The Bible provides a clear answer.

1. **Acknowledge** "For all have sinned and come short of the glory of God" (Romans 3:23). "God be merciful to me a sinner" (Luke 18:13).

2. **Repent** "Except ye repent, ye shall all likewise perish" (Luke 13:3) "Repent ye therefore, and be converted, that your sins may be blotted out" (Act 3:19).

3. **<u>Confess</u>** "If we confess our sins, He is faithful and just to forgive us our sins, and to cleanse us from all unrighteousness" (1 John 1:9). "If thous shalt confess with thy mouth the Lord Jesus, and shalt believe in thine heart that God hath raised Him from the dead, thou shalt be saved" (Roman 10:9).

4. **<u>Forsake</u>** "Let the wicked forsake his way, and the unrighteous man his thoughts; and let him return unto the Lord… for He will abundantly pardon" (Isaiah 55:7).

5. **<u>Believe</u>** "For God so loved the world, that He gave His only begotten Son, that whosoever believeth in Him should not perish, but have everlasting life" (John 3:16). "He that believeth and is baptized shall be saved; but he that believeth not shall be damned" (Mark 16:16).

6. **<u>Receive</u>** "He came unto His own, and His own received Him not. But as many as received Him, to

them gave He power to become the sons of God, even to them that believe on His name" (John 1:11,12).

Let's pray:

Dear Father God: I come before you in Jesus' name. I know that I am separated from You. I believe in my heart and confess with my mouth that He is Lord. I now renounce all sin in my life, any bitterness, unforgiveness, hatred or evil, and addictions. I renounce all involvement in the occult and mysterious. I command Satan's work to depart in Jesus' name. Forgive me Lord of these sins and cleanse my heart through the Blood of Jesus which was shed on the cross for me. Father, I ask you to give me the Holy Spirit and Lord Jesus Baptize me in the Holy Spirit. I receive the Baptism of the Holy Spirit by Faith. In Jesus' name, Amen.........

About The Author

C. Leo Young, Jr., is a choosen man by God for times like this. Having been nailed to the cross with Christ, I have died but Christ lives in me and I now live by faith in the Son of God who loved me and gave his life for me. I will give my life for him.